Common Co-Occurring Mental Health Conditions for

Individuals with Irritable Bowel Syndrome and Effective

Psychological Interventions

Nicole Mara Martinez, Psy.D., LCPC

Abstract

Irritable Bowel Syndrome (IBS) is one of the most common disorders that doctors see. It is a disorder that many individuals are not comfortable seeking treatment for due to the embarrassing nature of the associated symptoms. Primary symptoms include abdominal cramping, bloating and gas, and diarrhea or constipation. It is estimated that 10-20% of Americans suffer from symptoms of IBS. This is as high as one in five Americans. Many individuals who suffer from IBS can manage their symptoms with changes to their diet, lifestyle, and the reduction of stress. However, this study will seek to demonstrate that a high number of individuals suffering from IBS have co-occurring mental health disorders. The most common of these disorders appears to be anxiety and depression, with a high prevalence of alcohol and substance abuse. As stress is a trigger for exacerbating symptoms of IBS, mental health professionals can play a key role in providing a full range of treatments to the IBS patient. As this study will demonstrate, talk therapy, Cognitive Behavioral Therapy, hypnosis, and biofeedback have shown great promise and results when working with IBS patients. While it is evident that individuals with IBS greatly benefit from the aid of psychological services, this population remains to be extremely underserved. With this awareness, research, and education, it is hoped that mental health professionals will reach out to provide services to these individuals more in the near future.

Table of Contents

Introduction

This study seeks to identify the common co-occurring mental health conditions for individuals suffering from Irritable Bowel Syndrome (IBS). It will also seek to identify relevant and effective psychological treatments for individuals suffering from IBS. Available research suggests a potential link between IBS and certain common mental health conditions including: anxiety disorders, depression, adjustment disorders, neuroticism, somatization disorders, and conversion disorders. Research also suggests that talk therapy, cognitive behavioral therapy (CBT), hypnosis, and biofeedback are effective in the treatment of an individual with IBS. These potential links suggest that there is a need for further research in this area so that both clinical psychologists and medical practitioners can provide a full range of appropriate services for the patient.

According to the National Institutes of Health, Irritable Bowel Syndrome (IBS) is a "syndrome," which means a group of symptoms. The most common symptoms of IBS are abdominal pain or discomfort often reported as cramping, bloating, gas, diarrhea, and/or constipation. IBS affects the colon, or large bowel, which is the part of the digestive tract that stores stool. IBS is not a disease. It is a Functional Gastrointestinal Disorder (FGID), meaning that the bowel doesn't work, or function, correctly. IBS is the most common FGID. Multiple sources estimate that approximately 10-20% (or 25-40 million people) of the United States population suffers from IBS.

"Functional Gastrointestinal Disorders can affect any part of the gastrointestinal (GI) tract, including the esophagus, stomach, and intestines. They are disorders of function (how the GI tract works), not structural or biochemical abnormalities. As a result, x-rays, blood tests, and endoscopies can show essentially normal results. FGID's are also not psychiatric disorders, although stress and psychological difficulties can make FGID symptoms worse" (The UNC Center for Functional GI and Motility Disorders). This link helps to further illustrate the need for further research and collaborative efforts between mental and medical health professionals. With such a high prevalence of individuals suffering from IBS, it is shocking that this remains a nearly untouched area of psychology and health psychology. It is estimated that 25 million Americans have a functional GI disorder. "FGID's account for 40% of a gastroenterologists practice. 50-80% of persons with FGID's do not consult physicians, although they take over-the-counter medications and report significantly higher rates of job or school absenteeism and disability" (UNC Center for Functional GI and Motility Disorders).

Irritable Bowel Syndrome, the most common FGID, is altered bowel consistency combined with abdominal pain that is usually relieved with a bowel movement. The UNC Center

for Functional GI and Motility Disorders states that there are

three primary features of FGID's- motility, sensation, and

brain-gut dysfunction.

- **Motility** is the muscular activity of the GI tract. Normal

  motility is an orderly sequence of muscular contractions from the top to the bottom. In FGID's the motility is abnormal- there can be muscular spasms that can cause pain, and the contractions can be very rapid (diarrhea) or very slow (constipation).
- **Sensation** is how nerves of the GI tract respond to stimuli.

  In FGID's, the nerves are sometimes so sensitive that even normal contractions can bring on pain and discomfort.
- **Brain-gut dysfunction** relates to the disharmony in the way the brain and GI system communicate. With FGID's, the regulatory conduit between the brain and gut function may be impaired and this can lead to increased pain and bowel difficulties which can be worsened by stress.

This study will hopefully demonstrate a high-

concordance between IBS and various mental health

disorders mentioned previously. It will also hopefully

demonstrate how effective collaborative forms of mental

health therapies and medical treatments can be for the

individual. With high-concordance would come highly related psychological factors accompanying the physical manifestations of the disorder. It is believed that approximately 75-77% of medical complaints are psychosomatic and/or stress-related. Therefore, there is a great need for accurate diagnosis. The hope is that this study will demonstrate and emphasize the need for medical doctor's who treat these individuals to have some form of mental health screening tools, or refer the patients to a mental health professional for diagnosis. Mental health professionals need to be aware of services they can provide to potentially improve the IBS patient's quality of life. Research indicates that diet changes, medication (including antidepressants) and stress relief can significantly reduce symptoms of IBS. Mental health professionals could play a valuable role in medication management and stress reducing measures.

A number of areas of literature will be reviewed and utilized during the course of this study. Information regarding the symptoms, types, and courses of treatment for IBS will be covered. The topics of triggers, the difference between IBS and Inflammatory Bowel Disease (IBD), medical tests used in the diagnosis of IBS, the Rome Criteria, risk factors, and causes of IBS will be explored in further detail. This information will be gathered from sources including the National Institute of Health, and the American Journal of Gastroenterology. Research on the subject of Functional Gastrointestinal Disorders will be included with a focus on the research done by Olafur Palsson, Psy.D. Douglas A. Drossman, M.D., and William E. Whitehead, Ph.D. from the University Of North Carolina Center for Functional GI and Motility Disorders.

The study will briefly focus on what disease model the individual views their disease from (i.e. medical model, moral model, or disability model). The study will review literature describing common life stressors and psychosocial factors associated with IBS. Further, current research regarding links between anxiety, depression, stress, alcohol and substance abuse will be examined. Lastly, current research regarding potential interventions for the treatment of IBS will be studied including talk therapy (i.e. CBT and stress reduction), medications, and hypnosis. This information will be used to assess effective forms and outcomes of various treatment modalities. As IBS is a lifelong syndrome, meaning there is no cure, accurate diagnosis and identification of appropriate interventions by professionals becomes imperative to the individuals quality of life. With such a high numbers of individuals reportedly suffering from IBS, and the fact that this is an entirely underserved population, it becomes clear that this is an area requiring greater research and improved services provided by educated mental health professionals.

Procedures and Rationale

Irritable Bowel Syndrome has been shown to have high concordance with certain mental health conditions, especially anxiety, stress, and depression. Several forms of talk therapy and hypnosis have also been shown to be effective when it come to treating this syndrome. This information has been shown through prior research studies and articles written on the subject. Information regarding these issues was obtained by searching the EBSCOHOST database and typing in the key words and terms, "Irritable Bowel Syndrome," "treatments," and "mental health conditions."A systemic review of the literature on Irritable Bowel Syndrome from 1970 to 2008 was performed using EBSCOHOST. Full studies from a multitude of countries were identified and selected for inclusion. Case studies were excluded that focused on

Inflammatory Bowel Disease and those in which IBS

symptoms, treatment interventions, or co-occurring mental

health disorders were not included in the outcome measures.

Ethical Issues

There are no ethical issues to be concerned with as

there are no human subjects taking part in this literature

review. A major issue would be to respect the integrity of the

previous research while creating a unique and original review

which helps to provide new information for mental health

professional.

Literature Review

Overview of IBS

Irritable Bowel Syndrome is a disorder which causes cramping, abdominal pain, bloating, constipation, and diarrhea. It can cause an individual a great deal of discomfort for the individual as well as a certain degree of distress for the way it impacts an individuals functioning. IBS does not permanently harm the digestive tract or the intestines, and does not typically lead to more serious diseases, such as cancer, Crohn's disease, or colitis. IBS is not a disease. It is a functional disorder, meaning that the bowel does not work correctly. Most individuals find that they are able to manage their symptoms through a combination of diet, stress management techniques, and medications prescribed by a healthcare professional.

There are a certain percentage of individuals with IBS who find the disorder to be disabling. They find themselves struggling to work, participate in social activities, or take part in many activities that were once part of their daily lives. As was stated previously, "as many as 20% of the population (one in five Americans), present with symptoms of IBS, making it one of the most diagnosed disorders by doctors. It occurs more often in women (70% of cases) than in men, and it begins before the age of 35 in about 50% of people" (National Digestive Diseases Information Clearinghouse, p.3). IBS is responsible for over 3 million yearly visits to physicians. For years many doctors dismissed IBS as a psychological issue and negated that it was a physical problem, leaving few treatment options. However, due to recent research, medical professionals are beginning to understand that IBS is indeed caused by a physiological malfunction. A recent survey found that almost 33% of doctors view IBS as an emotional and not a physical problem. From this belief, many individuals with the disorder face negative stereotypes by healthcare professionals and may find they are less willing to seek help. Sophia Cariati (2003, p.4) believes that part of the problem lies in the fact that since IBS is a "functional disorder" which does not show up on blood tests or x-rays, it can not be objectively diagnosed. While patients report painful and often disabling symptoms, there are often no visible signs of the disorder. However, research shows that individuals suffering with IBS do have a significantly reduced quality of life which impacts their professional, social and personal lives. "Individuals with IBS visits doctors twice as often as healthy individuals and take significantly more prescription drugs."

Causes of IBS

Doctors are not certain what causes IBS. Nerves and muscles in the bowel are extremely sensitive and the muscles contract while the individuals eats, leading to cramping, bloating, gas, and diarrhea or constipation. So, one theory is that individuals with IBS are extremely sensitive to certain foods and stress. These foods and stressors would not bother most people. There is a belief that the immune system, which fights infection, may play a part in IBS as well. The individual with IBS has issues with motility or movement in the bowel. Recent research has discovered that serotonin is linked with normal gastrointestinal functioning. "Serotonin is a neurotransmitter, or chemical, that delivers messages from one part of your body to another. Ninety-five percent of the serotonin in your body is located in the GI tract, and the other 5 percent is found in the brain. Cells that line the inside of the bowel work as transporters and carry the serotonin out of the GI tract. People with IBS, however, have diminished receptor activity, causing abnormal levels of serotonin to exist in the GI tract. As a result, they experience problems with bowel movement, motility, and sensation – having more sensitive pain receptors in the GI tract" (National Digestive Diseases Information Clearinghouse, p.8). Also, since women are almost three times more likely to suffer from IBS, researchers believe that hormonal changes may play a role in the disorder.

It is believed that psychological factors also play a key role in IBS. HopkinsDigestion.com states that, "IBS and mental stress appear to be closely related, and people with depression and anxiety tend to be more susceptible to IBS. Studies also show an increased risk of IBS in women who have been physically or sexually abused." "Some studies suggest that IBS is caused by a malfunction in the way the brain and gut interact. These researchers theorize that the brain and spinal cord overreact to messages received from pain receptors in the gut. The brain then releases chemicals causing dramatic intestinal effects" (Cariati, S. 2003, p. 6). There is an "over or under activity of chemicals called neurotransmitters which regulate nerve impulses in the gut, and of one particular neurotransmitter: 5HT (serotonin)" (Crompton, 2001, p. 15). There is also more current research that links bacteria to IBS. "Researchers in California found excessive bacteria in 78% of IBS-sufferers tested. Treatment with antibiotics reduced or eliminated the bacteria in more than half of these patients leading to significant improvements in symptoms of IBS."

Symptoms of IBS

The signs and symptoms of IBS can vary widely from person to person and often resemble other diseases. The primary symptoms of IBS are abdominal pain or discomfort in the abdomen, which is often relieved by a bowel movement. Individuals can have chronic diarrhea, constipation, or both. Abnormal stool frequency such as greater than three bowel movements per day or less than three bowel movements per week. An individual can have white mucus in the stool, a swollen or bloated abdomen, gas, and symptoms may be more sever during women's menstrual periods. Some individuals find that their symptoms subside for several months and then return, while other's report that their symptoms appear to grow worse and worse over time. Some individuals may display only mild symptoms of IBS, while others find the disorder to be disabling. In some severe cases, an individuals IBS will not respond well to medical treatment. An individual suffering from abdominal pain must have the symptoms for a minimum of 12 weeks out of the previous 12 months. These twelve weeks do not have to be consecutive. "Bleeding, fever, weight loss, and persistent severe pain are not symptoms of IBS and may indicate other problems such as inflammation, or rarely, cancer" (National Digestive Disease Information Clearinghouse, p.12). Upper gastrointestinal (GI) symptoms are common amongst IBS patients with an estimated 25%-50% reporting symptoms of heartburn, satiety (feeling of fullness), abdominal fullness, intermittent upper abdominal discomfort or pain (dyspepsia), feelings of urgency to go to the restroom. There are also reports of non-gastrointestinal symptoms that may be "due to the coexistence or overlap of IBS with another condition such as fibromyalgia, chronic fatigue syndrome, or intestinal cystitis such as fatigue, muscle pain, sleep disturbances, sexual dysfunction, lower back pain, and headache" (American Gastroenterological Association, p.5). Symptoms which would indicate a condition more serious than IBS, and are not associated with IBS are blood in the stool, fevers, unexplained weight loss, and pain or diarrhea which wakes an individual from sleep.

Triggers of IBS

For reasons that are not clear, individuals with IBS have a strong reaction to stimulus that has seemingly no effect on others. "There are a number of factors known to aggravate, not cause, IBS symptoms. Large or fatty meals, some medications, excessive exercise, lack of sleep, menstruation, and stress are common triggers. Milk products, alcohol and excessive caffeine also tend to exacerbate the condition" (Cariati, S. 2003, p. 7). Other triggers are bloating from gas in the colon, wheat, rye, barley, chocolate, carbonated beverages, some fruits and vegetables, spicy foods, stress, conflict, or emotional upsets. "Researchers have found that women with IBS may have more symptoms during their menstrual periods, suggesting that reproductive hormones can worsen IBS problems. In addition, people with IBS frequently suffer from depression and anxiety, which can worsen symptoms. Similarly, the symptoms associated with IBS can cause a person to feel depressed or anxious" (National Digestive Disease Information Clearinghouse, p.12).

Diagnosis and Tests

A doctor may suspect an individual has IBS because of their symptoms. Specific symptoms, called the Rome Criteria, are often used to more accurately diagnose the disorder. Medical tests may also be done to ensure that someone does not have other health problems that cause similar symptoms. There is no specific test for IBS. However, a doctor may run tests to be sure that an individual does not have other diseases. A doctor will take a complete medical history, take a careful description of symptoms, and complete a physical examination at a bare minimum. Tests may include stool sampling, barium enemas, blood tests and x-rays to name a few. There is also the possibility that the doctor will conduct a colonoscopy or a lower gastrointestinal (GI) series.

If all test results are negative, a doctor can diagnose IBS based purely on the individual's symptoms. Some of these key symptoms include how often the individual experienced abdominal pain or discomfort, and if and when the pain subsides in relation to an individuals bowel movements. The International Foundation for Functional Gastrointestinal Disorders (IFFGD) states that, "because there are usually no physical signs to definitively diagnose irritable bowel syndrome, diagnosis is often a process of elimination. To help in this process, researchers have developed diagnostic criteria, known as the Rome criteria for IBS and other functional gastrointestinal disorders- conditions in which the bowel appears normal but doesn't function normally." Symptoms which would be red flags and indicate a more serious condition include the onset of symptoms after the age of 50, pain that awakens or interferes with sleep, blood in the stool, weight loss, fever, or recurrent vomiting.

Flexible sigmoidoscopy is a test which examines the lower part of the colon with a flexible lighted tube. A colonoscopy is when a small, flexible tube is used to view the entire length of the colon. A CT scan produces cross-sectional x-ray images of the internal organs. The scans of the abdomen and pelvis aid the doctor in ruling out various other conditions. Lactose intolerance tests look at the way your body digests lactase. If an individual does not produce this enzyme they may have symptoms similar to those of IBS. Blood tests can identify of an individual is suffering from Celiac disease which is a sensitivity to wheat protein which also has symptoms similar to IBS (IFFGD). Along with these there are two other tests which look for issues of malabsorption as opposed to IBS which includes a hydrogen breath test and gallbladder disease tests.

While professionals incorrectly thought that IBS was more of a psychological issue for years, research has clearly shown that it is indeed a very real, physical condition. While IBS is not a disease, but rather a functional disorder, it is characterized as a "brain-gut dysfunction" (Wikipedia). The Rome III Criteria is the current standard for diagnosing IBS. Wikipedia explains the need for the development of the Rome III criteria as follows:

The Rome Process is an international effort to define and

Categorize the functional gastrointestinal disorders, or FGID's,

(Of unknown cause) such as irritable bowel syndrome and

functional dyspepsia. This approach represents a substantial

change in thinking given that doctors have usually relied on

basic science and palpable evidence to diagnose all kinds of

ailments. More than half of gut disorders encountered by physicians are functional and there is no structural or chemical

explanation for them, so it was necessary to develop alternate methods to identify them. This process is akin to that followed by psychiatrists to categorize and diagnose psychiatric entities, which culminated in the DSM-IV criteria. These should not be "diagnoses of exclusion"; they demand a more positive approach. The Rome criteria have been evolving from the first set of criteria issued in 1989 (the Rome Guidelines for IBS) through the Rome Classification System for FGIDs (1990), or Rome-1, the Rome I Criteria for IBS (1992) and the FGIDs (1994), the Rome II Criteria for IBS (1999) to the recent Rome III Criteria (2006). "Rome II" and "Rome III" incorporated pediatric criteria to the consensus.

While physicians use a variety of tests and procedures to come to a diagnosis of IBS, the main symptom that must be present is abdominal pain. The Rome criteria is used after a thorough medical examination has taken place and in conjunction with or after laboratory tests have ruled out more serious disorders. "According to the Rome II committee and the Functional Brain Gut Research Group, IBS can be diagnosed based on at least 12 weeks, which need not be consecutive, of the preceding 12 months there was abdominal discomfort or pain that had two out of three of these features:"

- Relieved with defecation; and/or
- Onset associated with a change in frequency of stool; and/or
- Onset associated with a change in form (appearance) of stool

Symptoms that cumulatively support the diagnosis of IBS:

- Abnormal stool frequency (more than three bowel movements per
  day or less than three bowel movements per week);
- Abnormal stool form;
- Abnormal stool passage (straining, urgency, incomplete);
- Bloating or feeling of abdominal distention.

Supportive symptoms of IBS:

- Fewer than three bowel movements per week
- More than three bowel movements per day
- Hard or lumpy stools
- Loose or watery stools
- Straining during bowel movements
- Urgency (having to rush to the bathroom)
- Feeling of incomplete bowel movements
- Passing mucus during bowel movements

- Abdominal fullness, bloating, or swelling

Red flag symptoms which are not typical of IBS:

- Pain that awakens/ interferes with sleep
- Diarrhea that awakens/ interferes with sleep
- Blood in the stool (visible or occult)
- Weight loss
- Fever
- Abnormal physical examination

Risk Factors

There are a number of factors that can increase an individuals risk for developing IBS. While many people have occasional symptoms of IBS, you are the most likely to develop the disorder if you are young and female. IBS typically begins before the age of 35 (50% of the time), and three times as many women have the condition as men. It is believed, but unclear, that heredity plays a part in developing IBS. Stress is a significant risk factor for developing IBS. It is thought that individuals who suffer from IBS are more sensitive to stress. Another known cause is infectious gastroenteritis, or the stomach flu, with approximately 25% of cases leading to the development of IBS. Gastroenteritis is caused by a virus, bacteria, or parasite, and leads to diarrhea, vomiting, or both. "Researchers found that people who got gastroenteritis from salmonella poisoning were eight times more likely to develop IBS during the following year" (Suszynski, Marie 2008,p.17). Individuals with IBS are also believed to have more sensitive colons. These individuals colons either move to fast or too slow, causing diarrhea or constipation. Aberra identifies a number of "potential pathways that lead to the development of IBS:

> • Inflammation in the colon that damages the colonic walls and leads to the symptoms of IBS
> • Neuromuscular changes in the gastrointestinal (GI) tract that may lead to a change in the way the intestine moves its contents
> • Nerve damage in the GI tract itself, which leads to more
> sensitivity when the intestines are full and possibly a change in how the brain perceives movement and filling in the intestines
> • An overgrowth of bacteria or deficiency in beneficial bacteria in the gut
> • Abnormal levels of serotonin (which may regulate movement in the bowel)

Difference Between IBS and IBD

"The symptoms of IBS can overlap with those of inflammatory bowel disease (IBD), an umbrella term for Crohn's disease and ulcerative colitis. However, there are important differences between these disorders. Although both can cause pain, cramps, and digestive issues, IBD is associated with inflammation and ulceration in the intestines and rectum, a much more serious problem. And while an IBS diagnosis is based on symptoms, the inflammation in the GI tract of someone with IBD is clearly visible during an endoscopic exam" (Suszynski, M. 2007,p.18). Abdominal pain is the hallmark symptom of IBS, but it is also a symptom of many other conditions including inflammatory bowel disease (IBD).

Individual's with Crohn's disease have painful ulcers in their small and large intestines and sometimes have additional swelling of the rectum. Individuals with ulcerative colitis have ulcers in their rectum and large intestine. Inflammatory Bowel Disease's (IBD's) are much less common than IBS. While one in five individuals displays symptoms of IBS, only one in 200 people in the United States has an IBD. Both people with IBS and IBD's can experience symptoms of abdominal pain, cramping, bloating, and constipation and/or diarrhea. However, there are a few additional concerning symptoms for individuals with IBD's including any amount of rectal bleeding, fever, or weight loss.

When attempting to diagnose both IBS and an IBD, a doctor will typically use an endoscope to view the gastrointestinal tract of the individual. With someone with IBS, the doctor will not see any inflammation or obvious causes of the IBS symptoms or the illness. As previously mentioned, IBS is a "diagnosis of exclusion" (Aberra 2007, p.3). When a doctor views the gastrointestinal tract of an individual with an IBD, they will clearly see the inflammation that is causing the pain. A biopsy taking some of the cells to test from the inflamed area is then completed to confirm the diagnosis.

IBS and IBD's also have different treatment strategies as well. With IBS, doctors treat the symptoms. They may prescribe anti-diarrhea medications or fiber supplements, as well as dietary changes and stress reduction techniques. With IBD's doctors treat the inflammation. They might prescribe anti-inflammatory drugs such as corticosteroids (Suszynski 2008, p.20) to help reduce inflammation. Aberra states that in the most severe cases, doctors may prescribe immunosuppressant drugs.

Non-Therapy Treatments

Many individuals suffer with symptoms of IBS for quite some time before they seek medical help. It is estimated that up to 70% of individuals suffering with IBS do not receive medical treatment for their symptoms. While there is no cure for IBS, there are a number of thing that are believed to help reduce symptoms in individuals. Such treatments may include dietary changes, medications, and stress management techniques. Some dietary changes include removing foods from your diet such as fatty foods, milk products, alcohol, caffeinated drinks, and carbonated drinks. To identify other foods which might be issues, doctors may ask an individual to keep a food diary. It also might be suggested that the individual eat more frequent smaller meals throughout the day. Also, drinking plenty of fluids throughout the day, especially water, can be very useful. The doctor may suggest fiber supplements or laxatives for constipation and medicines which can decrease an individual's symptoms of diarrhea.

Doctors may also prescribe medications to aid with the symptoms. To start, doctors may prescribe antispasmodics to control abdominal spasms, anticholinergics, or antidepressants due to the high levels of serotonin present in the gut. Some research suggests that IBS could benefit from antibiotic treatments, but this remains unproven. It should also be noted that antispasmodics and antidepressants can increase constipation in an individual. Due to this fact, doctors might prescribe a medication that relaxes the muscles of the bladder and intestines. Unfortunately, these medications contain a mild sedative and can therefore become habit forming. Lotronex is prescribed for women with severe cases of IBS with their main symptom being diarrhea. This medicine has a history of causing serious side effects and is typically only prescribed as a last resort. Lotronex can cause serious constipation and/or decreased blood flow to the colon, causing serious side effects. On the other side, doctors may prescribe

Amitiza or Zelnorm for women suffering with sever constipation.

The National Institute of Diabetes and Digestive and Kidney Diseases (NIDDK) states, "some evidence suggests that IBS is affected by the immune system, which fights infection in the body. The immune system is affected by stress. For all these reasons, stress management is an important part of treatment for IBS. Stress management options include: stress reduction (relaxation) training and relaxation therapies such as meditation, counseling and support, regular exercise such as walking or yoga, changes to the stressful situations in one's life, and adequate sleep." Progressive muscle relaxation and deep breathing are also two interventions that have been shown to be somewhat effective for individuals. The International Foundation for Functional GI Disorders also suggests the use of herbs, including peppermint, acupuncture, to relax muscle spasms, and probiotics to introduce good bacteria into the intestines. An individual should educate themselves about the symptoms and options for treating IBS as well as seek out the others with

IBS for support. This might entail joining either an online or in-person support group.

Models of Disability

IBS can have a significant impact on a number of areas in an individual's life. It can affect their work, personal, and social lives. Suffering from IBS can alter the way an individual lives their lives and keep them from being more productive or participating in a number of activities that an individual once enjoyed. The Americans with Disabilities Act of 1990 defines disability as "a physical or mental impairment that substantially limits one or more major life activities." Various types of chronic conditions, whether an individual is born with them or they develop during a person's lifetime, qualify an individual as disabled. This being said, it is clear that individuals suffering from IBS fall under the title of disabled.

How the individual views their disability has a significant impact on if and the extent to which they will seek help for their disability. There are a number of different "models of disability," all of which come from a very different viewpoint and belief system about the individual's disability. The models that will be focused on are the medical model of disability, the social model of disability, the moral model of disability, and the empowering model.

The medical model of disability "is a model by which illness or disability is the result of a physical condition, is intrinsic to the individual (it is part of the individual's own body), may reduce the individual's quality of life, and causes clear disadvantages to the individual. As a result, curing or managing illness or disability revolves around identifying the illness or disability, understanding it and learning to control it and alter its course" (Wikipedia). As one can see, the role of the psychologist could be pivotal with this model. By aiding to treat the disability, the mental health professional can help to improve the individuals functioning and aid them in leading a more "normal" way of life. "The medical profession's responsibility and potential in this area is central."

The social model of disability states that there are societal "barriers, negative attitudes, and a feeling of exclusion (purposely or inadvertently) from other members of society. It recognizes that while some people have physical, sensory, intellectual, or psychological variations, which may sometimes cause individual functional limitations or impairments, these do not have to lead to disability, unless society fails to take account of and include people regardless of their individual differences" (Wikipedia). Due to the embarrassment and stigma associated with the symptoms of IBS, individuals may both exclude themselves from groups of people, or may be excluded due to lack of understanding. In this way, again, the mental health professional can aid the individual to face their illness, not feel stigmatized, teach them to educate others about their illness if desired, and seek support from others struggling with the same affliction.

The moral model of disability, as defined by Bowe in 1978, refers to "the attitude that people are morally responsible for their own disability. Such as viewing that their disability is a result of their own bad behavior. Bowe goes further to state that this attitude may be a "religious fundamentalist offshoot of the original animal roots of human beings when humans killed any baby that could not survive on its own in the wild." Quite the opposite, the empowering model of disability allows for the individual and those close to them to decide what course of treatment or services would most benefit an individual. This idea helps the mental health professional become a "service provider whose role is to offer guidance and carry out the client's decisions. In other words, this model empowers the individual to pursue their own goals." As one can see by the vast difference between these two models, a mental health professional can greatly aid the individual and make the difference between them feeling responsible for their illness or to make them feel as if they have control over their illness.

Quality of Life

Rosemarie Scolaro Moser (1986, p.109) states that, "What makes IBS such a nasty problem is the effect it can have on a person's social life, emotional well-being, and self-concept. Having IBS is not something one feels comfortable talking about, especially with others who do not understand it." These individuals have mixed feelings regarding the fact that they are not like the other people in their life who seem to live a more care-free existence, free from this type of distress and frustration with one's own body. When friends and family are unaware of the individuals condition, or do not fully understand it, they may interpret the individuals behavior as anger, seclusion, or moodiness. Rosemarie Scholar Moser pointed out an example of this in a case she "assessed, the parents were unaware of the disorder and interpreted their child's loss of control as acting out rather than as a psychophysiological response to emotional and environmental stress." "There is a high incidence of panic states or anxiety in these individuals, which may indicate that there is a neurohormonal or chemical basis" (Snape et al., 1976, p.329).

There have been a number of studies conducted assessing quality of life for individuals suffering form IBS. These studies addressed the impact IBS had on life factors including: activity, interference, body image, health worry, food avoidance, social reaction, sexual function, and relationships (Luscombe, 2000, p. 165). There are a number of quality of life assessment tools which address a number of areas that could negatively impact an individuals daily functioning or quality of life (QOL). These tools are utilized in the studies and the domains which they cover are described below. The Irritable Bowel Syndrome Questionnaire (IBSQ) addressed bowel function, fatigue, activity limitations, and emotional dysfunction. The Irritable Bowel Syndrome Quality of Life Questionnaire (IBSQOL) covers the nine domains of: emotional functioning, mental health, sleep, energy, physical functioning, diet, social role, physical role, and sexual relations. Lastly, the Functional Digestive Disorders Quality of Life Questionnaire (FDDQL) which addresses the eight domains of: daily activities, anxiety, diet, sleep, discomfort, coping, disease control, and stress.

It is evident that IBS can affect a many areas of an individual's life. It is also clear that depending on the severity of impairment in these areas, the individual could be profoundly impacted and be deemed to be suffering from a sub-standard quality of life. There are a number of domains addressed above that a mental health professional could be vital in treating. Some of these areas might include treatment to address the areas of dysphoria, activity interference, body image, health worry, relationships, sexual relations, emotional dysfunction, mental health, sleep, social functioning, anxiety, stress, and coping. These many areas of possible treatment and intervention clearly illustrate that the treatment of IBS is not merely a medical issue. To insure the highest quality of life, we as mental health professionals must treat the entire individual across a number of domains.

Psychopathology

Jeffrey Lackner, Psy.D. and his colleagues did a study in 2005 which investigated "the relationship between dysfunctional attitudes and the emotional unpleasantness of pain (pain affect) in a large sample (n=281) of severely affected patients with irritable bowel syndrome" (Lackner, et. Al, 2005, p. 151). The study demonstrated that individuals suffering from IBS who demonstrated negative thinking, also rated higher levels of pain affect than individuals who demonstrated healthier cognitions. Lackner goes onto address how cognitive therapy seeks to "eliminate automatic thoughts and underlying assumptions (core beliefs) that underlie excessive emotional or psychological reactions associated with GI symptoms." This is an example of the mind-body connection in IBS and how an individual's thoughts and beliefs can have a significant impact on the severity and course of their disorder. Individuals who perceive the worst case scenario appear to suffer from greater pain, more sick days, more frequent doctor visits, and less participation in enjoyable activities. As professionals, we can aim to dispute these faulty beliefs in an effort to help the individual see their situation more clearly, and inevitably lead a happier, more pain free life.

Carol Potera conducted a study which suggests that individuals who are unassertive are more likely to suffer from irritable bowel syndrome. This factor is especially prevalent in females who suffer from the syndrome. Carol Potera is in agreement with Jeffery Lackner, Psy.D. In the assumption that "most people who have IBS are submissive and nonassertive" (Potera, 2004, p.124), "they have difficulty making their needs known to others and being firm." This concept, that there are certain trait behaviors for individuals who suffer from IBS, helps to establish a framework from which to work from. A mental health professional can attempt to demonstrate the mind-body connection between feelings of loss of control or submission and symptom flair up. The therapist and client can work on feelings of worthiness as well as more assertive behaviors to aid in some alleviation of symptoms for the individual. The hope is that the individual can begin to see the connection between certain situations and behaviors and the flair up of their symptoms.

There has been a good amount of research to support the idea that individuals suffered from pre-existing psychiatric symptoms prior to developing IBS. Anxiety disorders are the most frequent example of this. A study conducted by Sykes, Lackner, Keefer, and Krasner, went as far to say that, "results support the theory that psychiatric symptoms, especially anxiety, play a role in the development of IBS" (Sykes, Et al, 2003, p. 361). They call this theory the "Psychosomatic Hypothesis," feeling that IBS is a "somatic expression of psychological problems." They also point out a contrary theory they refer to as the "Somatopsychic Hypothesis." This refers to the concept that individuals who suffer from IBS symptoms for an extended period of time are burdened with excessive stress, which can in turn lead to psychological problems (p. 363).

It is clear that looking at an individual entirely from either one of these perspectives could cause them to receive inadequate treatment. Looking at IBS as a purely psychological affliction could discount the medical treatment they receive. Looking at IBS from a purely medical perspective could cause a failure to receive pertinent conjunctive psychological treatment. Taking this into consideration, the authors of this study felt it relevant to refer to IBS as a psychophysiological disorder, taking into account both factors as equally important.

Individuals who suffer from IBS show higher scores on scales 1, 2, 3, and 7 on the MMPI than normal controls (Blachard & Scharff, 2002, p. 726). Scale 1 is the Hypochondrias scale (Hs). A high score on this scale depicts an individual who is unrealistically concerned with physical complaints. Scale 2 is the Depression scale (D). High scores

on this scale indicate an individual who is unhappy,

depressed, and pessimistic. Scale 3 is the Hysteria scale (Hy).

A high score on this scale indicates a person who focuses on

vague physical symptoms to avoid dealing with severe

psychological stress. Scale7 is the Psychasthenia scale (Pt).

High scores on this scale indicate an individual who is tense,

rigid, anxious, and may have obsessive thoughts and

compulsive behaviors.

Anxiety and Stress

Anxiety Disorders are the most common mental health

disorder to be present prior to the onset of symptoms of IBS.

Anxiety can lead an individual to perceive a greater risk of

health problems and may actually increase the manifestation

of symptoms associated with IBS. "Individuals with IBS differ

from healthy groups in levels of anxiety and depression, in

levels of recent and current symptoms and on measures of

bodily preoccupation and disease phobia" (Crane & Martin,

2004, p.234). Individuals with IBS have significantly higher scores on the State-Trait Anxiety Inventory (STAI) than normal controls. Anxiety is found to be a greater problem than depression in individuals suffering with IBS. "Worry does seem to predict gastrointestinal symptom severity" (Keefer, et. Al, 2005, p.163). There are individuals who believe that IBS is "a physiological expression of an affective disorder" (Toner, 1990, p.6). Catherine Patch points out that the gastrointestinal tract is extremely sensitive to adrenaline (2001, p.2). This is a hormone that the system produces when it is "excited, frightened, or anxious." Panic Disorder is also relatively common among individuals who suffer from IBS.

DSM-IV-TR has certain criteria individuals often display when suffering from Anxiety Disorder, these are:

- Excessive anxiety about a number of events or activities,

    occurring more days than not, for at least 6 months

- The person finds it difficult to control the worry

- Restlessness or feeling keyed up or on edge

- Being easily fatigued

- Difficulty concentrating or their mind going blank

- Irritability

- Muscle tension

- Sleep disturbance

An individual who suffers from anxiety is often worried about being embarrassed in public. An individual suffering from IBS may be doubly nervous about this due to possible symptom flare up in public. They may become preoccupied with feelings of worry about this and therefore exacerbate their symptoms even further. These individuals often have numerous physical complaints, especially gastrointestinal symptoms.

Studies show that individuals suffering from IBS perceive their risk of susceptibility to health related issues to be greater than individuals not suffering with IBS. Crane and Martin conducted such a study which showed that individuals suffering with IBS have an increased perception that they will develop unrelated health problems, as well as "non-health physical risks (mugging, traffic accident), both when making estimates for themselves and for an average person of their own age" (2004, p.216). When an individual is pre-occupied with, or views their health risks as greater than they are in reality, they are more likely to "contribute to IBS-related illness behavior, and may increase vulnerability to the development of other functional disorders." While stress does not cause IBS, people with IBS are more likely to have symptom flare ups with increased stress levels. Signals from the brain, the hypothalamus, send messages to the gut every second causing increased sensitivity. So, it is to be believed that increased levels of daily stress can account for increased gastrointestinal symptoms.

Depression

Individuals with IBS typically have higher scores on the Beck Depression inventory than normal controls. Often IBs suffered meet the criteria for major depressive disorder, however, they do not consider themselves depressed or report symptoms of depression to the doctor, or at least do not consider the symptoms they are reporting to be associated with depression. "70-90% of individuals who seek medical treatment for IBS may have psychiatric co-morbidity, most commonly mood disorders, anxiety disorders and somatization disorders" (Sharma, et. al., 2003, p.1). Major depression is one of the most prevalent mood disorders that individuals with IBS suffer from. The presence of major depression is thought to exacerbate physical symptoms of IBS. "Patients with major depression and IBS were more likely to report symptoms of back pain, weakness, and nocturnal abdominal pain as compared to patients with major depression who did not have IBS" (p.1). Another study conducted in Ireland estimates that between 42-60% of individuals suffering with IBS also have anxiety or depression. The study found that individuals suffering from IBS and depression were more likely to demonstrate pain in their lower back, thighs, and have extreme levels of fatigue (Houston, 2006, p.1). This supports the finding that the link between depression and IBS can severely increase the manifestation of physical symptoms in an individual.

The DSM-IV-TR characterizes individuals suffering from major depressive disorder to have the majority of these symptoms present:

- Depressed mood most of the day, nearly every day, as indicated by either subjective report or observation made by others.

- Markedly diminished interest or pleasure in all, or almost all, activities most of the day, nearly every day.

- Significant weight loss when not dieting or weight gain, or decrease or increase in appetite nearly every day.

- Insomnia or hypersomnia nearly every day.

- Psychomotor agitation or retardation nearly every day.

- Fatigue or loss of energy nearly every day.

- Feelings of worthlessness or excessive or inappropriate guilt nearly every day.

- Diminished ability to think or concentrate, or indecisiveness, nearly every day.

- Recurrent thoughts or death, recurrent suicidal ideation without a specific plan, or a suicide attempt or a specific plan for committing suicide.

It is clear that suffering from wither IBS or major depression can be difficult enough for an individual, but the two coupled together can make life fairly unbearable for an individual. IBS can exacerbate weight loss, fatigue, depressed feelings, and marked loss of interest in activities one once enjoyed due to fear of symptom flair ups. This is yet another example of the dire need for medical and psychological professionals to work together to treat individuals suffering from IBS, particularly those with co-occurring mental health disorders.

Trauma, Alcohol and Substance Abuse

Individuals with IBS typically report high levels of physical, emotional, and sexual abuse. They have this in common with a large number of substance abusers. Such experiences with trauma "may lead to reductions in perceived control, which in turn may be associated with lowered perception of preventability of health problems, and hence increased perceptions of susceptibility/ perceived risk" (Kulik &Mahler, 1987). It is believed that the relationship between gastrointestinal disorders and a history of physical and/or sexual abuse is very high. Peter Salmon, Katherine Skaife, and Jonathon Rhodes conducted a study in which they investigated the role of dissociation and somatization in linking abuse to IBS. "By comparison with physically diseased patients, patients with IBS recalled more sexual abuse as children and adults, more physical abuse as children, and more psychological abuse as adults. They were more anxious and depressed, and somatized and dissociated more." They found that dissociation causes an increase in physical symptoms (2002, p.1).

Individuals suffering from trauma can suffer from either Post Traumatic Stress Disorder (PTSD) or Acute Stress Disorder. Individuals often relive the traumatic event on a recurrent basis, or go to great lengths in order to avoid these unpleasant thoughts and feelings associated with the traumatic event. These individuals are often likely to turn to drugs and alcohol as a means of avoiding this pain and thereby putting themselves in an altered state of consciousness. Other individuals are so fixated on these events and relive them on such a frequent basis that they cause themselves physical distress. This distress is often manifested in gastrointestinal symptoms. The recurrent thoughts send messages from the brain to the gut and cause symptoms to increase.

Studies have found a significant link between IBS and alcohol and drug abuse. It is believed that anywhere from 29-42% of individuals who suffer from alcohol or substance dependence may have IBS as well. This is further confounded by the fact that anywhere from 70-90% of substance abusers also have some form of trauma history. This puts into perspective the fact that many individuals may suffer from IBS, alcohol and/or substance abuse, as well as a history of trauma or abuse. It is believed that "IBS is common and frequently under diagnosed in patients with alcohol abuse or dependence" (Masand, Sousou, Gupta, & Kaplan, 1998), p.514).

Interventions

An important first step in the psychological treatment of individuals with IBS is to provide them with psychoeducation. This would involve explaining to individuals the personal triggers and cues they may have that cause them to have flare ups and increase their symptoms of IBS. These can be emotional, behavioral, physical, or cognitive. How an individual is feeling, their automatic thoughts, or the actions they take can play a significant role in the frequency and intensity of their symptoms. Along with this, the individual should be educated on the workings of the GI system so that they might better understand the connection between their thoughts, feelings, and the physical manifestation of their symptoms. It is important that they understand that while their illness and symptoms are not "all in their head," that their thoughts and feelings, as well as the presence of symptoms of anxiety, depression, and stress, can greatly impact their physical well-being.

Edward Blanchard and Howard Malamood feel that there are four different classes of psychological treatments that are effective for IBS, there are "brief psychodynamic psychotherapy, hypnotherapy, multi-component cognitive-behavioral treatment regimens, and cognitive therapy" (1996, p. 241). The benefits from these types of treatments have been shown to maintain effectiveness for up to four years for individuals. Another study conducted by Concepcion Fernandez and Isaac Amigo found that stress management training and contingency management training proved to be effective forms of treatment as well (2006, p.21). Specific interventions will be discussed in more detail, but one fact seems apparent, determining an individual's suitability for treatment and the type of intervention that would be most beneficial to them is paramount. Since the course and severity of symptoms vary with such great degree from person to person, interventions should be as unique as the individual.

Individuals who are thought to be appropriate for stress management training are taught skills such as progressive muscle relaxation. They were also taught how their reactions to the circumstances in their lives can worsen their symptomology. In the Fernandez and Amigo study the patients were faced with imagined and real situations and encouraged to use self-instruction, problem-solving, progressive muscle relaxation, and were asked to keep weekly symptoms to track the effectiveness of the strategies (p.292). Contingency management training aims "to teach the patients, and whenever possible, other people involved in their daily lives, to put into practice behavioral patterns which are more appropriate to IBS symptoms and the situations which aggravate them and, at the same time, to avoid inappropriate behavior (e.g. isolation, dependence, delegation, overprotection) (2006, p.292).

Relaxation-training, meditation, stress management procedures, and hypnosis have been shown to "produce sustained reductions in somatic symptoms" (Weber, McCallum, & Lancet 1992, p.5). Psychotherapy is also shown to be helpful to patients who are motivated for relief as well as those with underlying symptoms of depression and anxiety. There are a number of studies that imply that individuals often receive greater benefit and increased symptom reduction from psychological interventions over routine medical care.

Cognitive therapy appears to be an extremely effective intervention for individuals suffering from IBS. Individuals who receive cognitive therapy show reductions in physical symptoms, as well as symptoms of depression and anxiety at a three month follow-up after treatment. The effectiveness of cognitive therapy has been replicated over numerous studies with different participants and new therapists each time. Similar results were reached with each subsequent study. This implies that this is an effective and highly reliable form of treatment for individuals with IBS.

Barbara Greene and Edward Blanchard did a study examining the effectiveness of cognitive therapy for individuals with IBS. The study compared a group of individuals who received intensive cognitive therapy for eight weeks versus a group who participated in daily GI symptom monitoring. The group who received the cognitive therapy showed significant symptom reduction in 80% of participants. Only 10% of the group participating in symptom monitoring showed improvement. The results continued to hold at a three month follow-up. "Within the cognitive therapy group, GI symptom reduction correlated significantly with increases in positive and reductions in negative automatic thoughts" (Greene & Blanchard 1994, p. 576). A study done at King's College London School of Medicine found that individuals who suffered from IBS and participated in various forms of talk therapy for a period of 12 weeks, reported a 40% improvement in their symptoms (Andrews, 2006, p.42). This is an important point as individuals who only took medications to manage their symptoms and did not participate in any form of talk therapy only reported a 16% improvement in their symptoms. There was also a study conducted in Australia in which individuals participated in 8 weeks of CBT. After the eight week period had ended, more than half of the participants no longer met the Rome diagnostic criteria for IBS, they showed significant improvements in levels of distress, and anxiety and depression symptoms were greatly reduced (Boyce, et.al, 2000, p.300).

These studies help illustrate the benefits and importance of psychological and medical treatment for optimum symptom reduction.

"Cognitive behavioral therapy (CBT) for IBS symptoms includes assessment and treatment of the behavioral, cognitive, and physiological phenomena associated with the gastrointestinal symptoms and illness behavior. Illness behavior is a term that refers to the way people perceive and react to somatic sensations that might signify disease" (Levy & Walker 2005, p. 137). The authors discuss how social learning theory can provide a better understanding of how illness behavior begins. Individuals, especially children, can receive "social rewards such as increased attention, avoidance of unpleasant work or social situations, or financial compensation (p. 138). The individual may receive other positive consequences including "expressions of support, caring, or concern, or decreased negative events such as fewer demands for participation in taxing activities" (p.139). These factors over time may contribute to illness behaviors. This being said, CBT should address issues of learned behavior and help individuals to learn new ways of thinking, particularly to see the benefits of symptom reduction over the attention they receive for displaying illness behavior.

Based on Beck's model, Cognitive Therapy can help individuals to learn to identify "anxiety-provoking dysfunctional thoughts, expectations and assumptions, both as they relate to IBS and in general terms." Individuals can then be taught to "challenge or modify errors in their thinking to produce more accurate, rational and helpful thoughts" (Boyce et. al., 2000, p.303). It can help individuals to see the difference between their symptoms when they display negative thoughts and beliefs in regards to their health and the severity of their illness, and when they develop a positive outlook and belief system in regards to managing illness. Individuals displaying more severe symptomolgy may feel overwhelmed and have little faith in their ability to get better, manage their illness, or lead a normal productive life. An individual who believes that they can implement changes in their daily living to manage symptoms, and utilize valuable techniques to reduce stress and alleviate suffering, may display less severe symptomology. In these cases, it is clear how effective cognitive therapy can be, specifically as it relates to an individuals automatic thoughts and belief system. The cognitive techniques of "distraction, thought stopping, worry sessions, coping self-statements, and cognitive restructuring" can be extremely beneficial in these cases (p. 304).

"The goal of treatment is to shift the patient from a medical view that the IBS condition is largely outside of the person's control to a view that the symptoms are under significant patient control" (Toner, Segal, Emmott,& Myran, 2000, p. 202). The authors further discuss the confounding issues with women suffering from IBS. They discuss the female gender role and some individual's propensity to act passively, making them more likely to feel powerless over their illness. It can be difficult, but not impossible, to teach these individuals that they can indeed have control over their body and their overall well-being. Males tend to demonstrate the belief that they have some degree of control of their bodies and their physical well-being. This helps explain the fact that 70% of individuals suffering from IBS are females. Also, as caretakers, women are more likely to care for others before tending to their own needs, where males more immediately deal with their discomfort and implement strategies to ease their suffering.

Olafur S. Palsson is the foremost expert in the treatment of IBS using hypnotherapy. He admits that while hypnosis may not be the "most suitable option for all patients, it has some advantages which makes it an attractive option for many IBS sufferers with chronic and severe symptoms" (Palsson, O. 2008, p.4). Some facts and figures that Olafur Palsson provides on his website include the following:

- It is the most successful treatment approach for chronic IBS. The response rate to treatment is 80% and better in most published   studies to date.

- The treatment often helps individuals who have failed to get improvements with other methods.

- It is a uniquely comfortable form of treatment; relaxing, easy and generally enjoyable.

- It utilizes the healing power of the person's own mind, and is generally completely without negative side effects.

- The treatment sometimes results in improvement in other symptoms or problems such as migraine or tension headaches, along with the improvement in IBS symptoms.

- The beneficial effects of the treatment last long after the end of the course of treatment. According to research, individuals who improve from hypnosis treatment for IBS can generally look forward to years of reduced bowel symptoms.

There is a good deal of published research supporting the effectiveness of hypnotherapy over other psychological interventions for the treatment of IBS symptoms. One such study by Tara Galovski and Edward Blanchard found that not only did hypnosis improve symptoms of abdominal pain, constipation, and flatulence, but it improved state and trait anxiety scores as well. These results held true at a two month follow up to the study (1998, p. 219).

Hypnotherapy has been a leading treatment for IBS in Britain since the 1980's, but has been slow to catch on in the United States. They found that hypnotherapy was extremely effective in treating severe cases and even treatment resistant strains of IBS. Many individuals no longer required the need for medication to manage the illness after undergoing a series of hypnotherapy sessions. Hypnotherapy often times has a stigma in the United States where individuals relate it to stage performers who make individuals act in embarrassing manners. Another study conducted at the University Hospital of South Manchester in England followed 200 female IBS sufferers over a 6 years period after receiving three months worth of hypnotherapy. 71% of the women reported a significant improvement in their symptoms, and their symptoms had no recurrence 6 years later (Levine, 2004, p.51). Researchers at Edinburgh University found that the biggest improvement from hypnotherapy sessions was seen in women.

Hypnotherapy appears to not only help to significantly lessen the occurrence of symptoms of IBS, it concurrently lessens anxiety levels as well. The Research conducted at Edinburgh University supports this finding as well. Further a study found in the Journal of Alternative and Complementary

Medicine found improvement in "all major symptoms of IBS, extracolonic symptoms, quality of life, anxiety, and depression" (Gholamrezaeri, Ardenestani, & Emanmi, 2006, p. 517). Olafur Palsson found similar results through his years of research. In numerous studies he measures somatization, anxiety, and depression. He found that large decreases in the prevalence of somatization and psychological distress with the addition of hypnotherapy. He concluded that, "Hypnosis improves IBS symptoms through reductions in psychological distress and somatization" (Palsson, Turner, Johnson, Burnett & Whitehead, 2002).

Edward Blanchard has conducted numerous studies regarding effective psychological treatments for individuals suffering from IBS. In one such critical review he states that, "there is no compelling evidence for the superiority of one approach over the other" (Blanchard 2005, p.118). This alludes to the fact that there is no definitive intervention that has been proven to be successful in all patients with IBS. This point only strengthens the thought that interventions should be unique and tailored to meet individual needs and symptoms.

While one individual may greatly benefit from relaxation techniques to manage symptom flares ups and stress management techniques to prevent the onset of symptoms, other individuals might greatly benefit from talk therapy to combat faulty beliefs and address their view of the disease model.

Discussion

The purpose of this review was to identify the most common co-occurring mental health conditions that people suffering with IBS have. It also sought to identify the most effective psychological interventions mental health professionals can use to treat individuals suffering from IBS. From the review of previous research some themes and information has become clear. These topics include the need for professionals across fields to work together, the link between IBS and mental health conditions, the need for work with these individuals to become a focus in psychological services, and the need to identify the most effective treatments for each individual.

Medical and psychological professionals need to work in conjunction with one another to provide the most complete and effective range of services for individuals suffering from IBS. This means identifying an all encompassing plan to treat both the physical and mental health conditions individuals with IBS so often suffer from. Psychological work with individuals with IBS appears to be a growth industry for mental health professionals as 10-20% of the population suffer with symptoms of IBS. This is a population that is often underserved or not served at all by mental health professionals even though it affects so many. Of the 10-20% of the population who suffer from IBS, it is believed that 70-90% of these individuals also suffer from conditions such as anxiety, depression, somatization disorders, and alcohol and substance abuse issues. These factors indicate a need for further research as well as education and training for mental health professionals to work with this population.

There appears to be genuine link between the development of IBS and pre-existing mental health conditions. There is a large number of individuals with anxiety disorders as well as depression who go on to develop symptoms of IBS. There also appears to be a link between the onset of symptoms of IBS and the new development of mental health conditions. The most common of these mental health conditions are anxiety disorders, depression, and alcohol and substance abuse issues. Individuals who are suffering with the varied symptoms of IBS find themselves with increased levels of stress, feelings of depression, not being able to participate in activities they once enjoyed for fear of a flare up, and often isolate themselves out of embarrassment.

Women suffer from IBS at disproportionate amounts to men (70% vs. 30%). This overwhelming difference in effect rates suggests a needs for further research. This also might suggest a need to look at female focused psychological interventions as there are likely slight differences between responses to therapy and psychological interventions between males and females. For example, studies indicate that females are slightly more open to hypnotherapy than men, but there is no conclusive evidence to support this fact.

CBT, hypnosis, talk therapy, and biofeedback appear to be the most effective psychological interventions for individuals suffering from IBS. As mentioned previously, there is no proof that one intervention is more effective than another, so deciding which approach to use should be decided on an individual basis and by what the client seems to respond most favorably to. In terms of hypnosis, we need to work to break the stigma in the United States of using hypnotherapy to treat IBS as it not only reduces physical symptoms, but reduces levels of anxiety, depression, and somatization while improving quality of life. The use of hypnotherapy for the treatment of IBS is much more readily accepted in the United Kingdom than it is in the United States.

Studies of psychological conditions associated with IBS, effective interventions, and how we can help as mental health professionals must continue to be done as most of the research in this field was conducted in the late 1990's. Much has been learned about this condition and its treatment since that time and much can be taught to both new and seasoned professionals to help these individuals live with the best quality of life possible.

References

Aberra, Fatan (2009). Cited in article by Marie Suszynski.

http://www.pennmedicine.org/WagForm/MainPage.aspx?config=provider&P=PP&ID=9296

American Digestive Health Foundation.

http://www.fdhn.org/wmspage.cfm?parm1=27

American Gastroenterological Association.

Http://www.gastro.org/wmspage.cfm?parm1=2

American Psychiatric Association. *Diagnostic and statistical manual of mental disorders, 4th edition.* Washington, DC: American Psychiatric Association, 1994.

American Psychological Association (1996).

Psychological interventions found to benefit People who seek treatment for Irritable Bowel Syndrome.

Americans with Disabilities Act (1990).

http://www.ada.gov/.

Andrews, Julie (2006). Positive thoughts help IBS.

Prevention, 58, 5, p. 42.

Blanchard, Edward (2005). A critical review of cognitive, behavioral, and cognitive-behavioral therapies for Irritable Bowel Syndrome. *Journal of Cognitive Psychotherapy, 19,* 2, p. 101-123.

Blanchard, Edward (2005). Cognitive psychotherapy and

Irritable Bowel Syndrome: Introduction to the special

issue. *Journal of Cognitive Psychotherapy, 19,* 2, p. 99-100.

Blanchard, E. & Malamood, H. (1996). Psychological

treatment of Irritable Bowel Syndrome. *Professional :*

Research and Practice, 27, 3, pp. 241-244.

Blanchard, E. & Scharff, Lisa (2002). Psychosocial

aspects of and treatment of Irritable Bowel Syndrome in adults

and recurrent abdominal pain in children. *Journal of*

Consulting

and Clinical Psychology, 70, 3, pp. 725-738.

Bogalo, Laura & Moss-Morris, Rona (2006). The

effectiveness of homework tasks in an Irritable Bowel

Syndrome self-management programme. *New Zealand*

Journal of Psychology, 35, 3, pp. 120-125.

Boyce, P., Gilchrist, J., Talley, N., Rose, D., & Boyce, P.

(2000). Cognitive-behavior Therapy as a treatment for Irritable

Bowel Syndrome: A pilot study. *Australian & New Zealand*

Journal of Psychiatry, 34, 2, p. 300-309.

Cariarti, Sophia (2003). Irritable Bowel Syndrome More

than an Irritation. *Society for Women's Health Research.*

Cohen, S. & Morris, L. (2004). Mind over IBS. *Shape, 23,*

8, p.97.

Crane, Catherine & Martin, Maryanne (2004). Risk

perception in individuals with Irritable Bowel Syndrome:

Perceived susceptibility to health and non-health threats.

Journal of Social & Clinical Psychology, 23, 2, pp. 216-239.

Creed, F., Guthrie, E., Ratcliffe, J., Fernandes, L., Rigby, C.,

Tomenson, B., Read, N., & Thompson, D., (2005). Does

psychological treatment help only those patients with severe

Irritable Bowel Syndrome who also have concurrent

psychiatric disorder? *Australian & New Zealand Journal of*

Psychiatry, 39, 9, p. 807-815.

Crompton, Simon (2001). Is IBS all in the mind? *Times UK,* pp.14-

17. Disorders of the lower digestive tractHopkinsDigestion.com.

Digestive Disorders, Jan. 2006, pp.45-81

Fernandez, C. & Amigo, I. (2006). Efficacy of training in stress and contingency management in cases of Irritable Bowel Syndrome. *Stress and Health, 22,* pp. 286-295.

Foxhall, Katherine (2001). APA book notes: An almost untouched area of health psychology: New book says many patients with Irritable Bowel Syndrome could Be helped by psychological treatment, but few psychologists treat the disorder. *Monitor on Psychology, 32,* 5, pp. 64-65.

Galovski, T. & Blanchard, E. (1998). The treatment of Irritable Bowel Syndrome with hypnotherapy. *Applied Psychophysiology &Biofeedback, 23,* 4, p. 219-232.

Gholamrezael, A., Khanpour Ardestani, S., & Hasan Emami, M. (2006). Where does Hypnotherapy stand in the management of Irritable Bowel Syndrome? A Systematic review. *The Journal of Alternative and Complimentary Medicine, 12,* 6, pp. 517-527.

Greene, B., & Blanchard, E. (1994). Cognitive therapy for Irritable Bowel Syndrome. *Journal of Consulting and Clinical Psychology, 62,* 3, pp. 576-582.

Houston, Mulris (2006). Stress implicated as factor in IBS. *Irish Times,* 3/14/2006.International Foundation for Functional Gastrointestinal Disorders.

http://www.iffgd.org/. Irritable Bowel Syndrome. *Wikepedia, http://en.wikipedia.org/wiki/Irritable_bowel_syndrome*

Keefer, L., Sanders, K., Sykes, M., Blanchard, E., Lackner, J., & Krasner, S. (2005). Towards a better understanding of anxiety in Irritable Bowel Syndrome: A Preliminary look at worry and intolerance of uncertainty. *Journal of Cognitive Psychotherapy, 19,* 2, pp. 163-172.

Kelly, A. & Martin, A. (2004). Got IBS? Get hypnotized- it just might help. *Health, 18,* 2, p. 56-60.

Kraft, tom & Kraft, David (2007). Irritable Bowel Syndrome: Symptomatic treatment versus integrative psychotherapy. *Contemporary Hypnosis, 24,* 4, pp. 161-177.

Kulik, J.A., & Mahler, H.I. (1987). Health status, perceptions of risk,

   And prevention interest for health and non-health problems.

   Health Psychology, 6, 15-27.

Lackner, J., Gellman, R., Gudleski, G., Sanders, K., Krasner, S., &

   Blanchard, E. (2005). Dysfunctional attitudes, gender, and

   psychopathology as predictors of pain affect in patients with

   Irritable Bowel Syndrome. *Journal of Cognitive*

   Psychotherapy, 19, 2, pp. 151-161.

Lackner, Jeffrey (2005). No brain, no gain: The role of cognitive

   processes in Irritable Bowel Syndrome. *Journal of Cognitive*

   Psychotherapy, 19, 2, p. 125-136.

Lackner, J., Morley, S., Dowzer, C., Mesmer, C, & Hamilton, S.

   (2004). Psychological treatments for irritable bowel syndrome:

   A systematic review and meta-analysis. *Journal of Consulting*

   and Clinical Psychology, 72, 6, pp. 1100-1113.

Levine, Lois (2004). The mind-over-belly plan for IBS. *Prevention,*

   56, 5, p.51.

Levy, R., Cain, K., Jarrett, M., & Heitkemper, M. (1997). The relationship between daily life stress and gastrointestinal symptoms in women with Irritable Bowel Syndrome. *Journal of Behavioral Medicine, 20,* 2, pp. 177-193.

Levy, R. & Walker, L. (2005). Cognitive behavior therapy for the treatment of recurrent abdominal pain. *Journal of Cognitive Psychotherapy, 19,* 2, p. 137-149.

Lewis, Carol (2001). Irritable Bowel Syndrome: A poorly understood disorder. *U.S. Food and Drug Administration FDA Magazine, 401,* July-August, pp. 1-10.

Luff, Steven (2004). Gut check. *Vegetarian Times, 324,* pp. 75-78.

Luscombe, Faye A. (2000). Health-related quality of life and associated psychosocial factors in Irritable Bowel Syndrome: A review. *Quality of Life Research: An International Journal of Quality of Life Aspects of Treatment, Care & Rehabilitation, 9,* 2, pp. 161-176.

Martin, R., Davis, G., Baron, R., Suls, J., & Blanchard, E. (1994). Specificity in social support: Perceptions of helpful and unhelpful provider behaviors among Irritable Bowel Syndrome, headache, and cancer patients. *Health Psychology, 13,* 5, pp. 432-439.

Masand, P., Sousou, A., Gupta, S., & Kaplan D. (1998). Irritable Bowel Syndrome (IBS) and alcohol abuse and dependence. *American Journal of Drug and Alcohol Abuse, 24,* 3, pp. 513-521.

Medical Model of Disability. *Wikepedia, http://en.wikipedia.org/wiki/Medical_model_of_disability*

Mikocka-Walus, A., Turnball, D., Andrews, J., Moulding, N., Wilson, I., Harley, H., Hetzel, D., & Holtmann, G. (2008). Psychological problems in gastroenterology outpatients: A South Australian experience. Psychological co-morbidity in IBD, IBS, and hepatitis C. *Clinical Practice and Epidemiology in Mental Health, 15,* 4, pp. 1-8.

Moral Model of Disability. *Wikepedia, http://en.wikipedia.org/wiki/Disability*

Moser, Rosmarie Scholaro (October 1986). Irritable Bowel Syndrome: A misunderstood psychophysiological affliction. *Journal of Counseling & Development, 65,* 2, p.108-109.

National Institute of Diabetes and Digestive Diseases and Kidney

Diseases (NIDDK). National Digestive Diseases Information Clearinghouse (NDDIC)

http://digestive.niddk.nih.gov/ddiseases/pubs/ibs_ez/index.htm

Palsson, O.S. (2008). www.IBShypnosis.com.

Palsson, O.S., Turner, M.J., Johnson, D.A., Burnett, C.K., & Whitehead, W.E. (2002). Hypnosis treatment for severe irritable bowel syndrome: investigation of mechanism and effects on symptoms. *Digestive Diseases Science, 47*, 11, pp. 2605-2014.

Patch, Catherine (2001). Bowel disorder can lead to depression. *Toronto Star,* 1/18/2001.

Payne, Annette & Blanchard, Edward (1995). A Controlled comparison of cognitive therapy and self-help support groups in the treatment of Irritable Bowel Syndrome. *Journal of Consulting and Clinical Psychology, 63,* 5, pp. 779-786.

Potera, Carol (2004). The IBS-prone personality. *Shape, 24,* 1, p. 124.

Rome Criteria for Diagnosis.

http://www.helpforibs.com/footer/rome_guidelines.asp

Rome Process. *Wikepedia,*

http://en.wikipedia.org/wiki/Rome_Process

Rutter, Claire & Rutter, Derek (2002). Illness representation, coping and outcome in irritable bowel syndrome (IBS). *British Journal of Health Psychology, 7,* pp. 377-391.

Salmon, P., Skaife, K., & Rhodes, J. (2003). Abuse, dissociation, and somatization in Irritable Bowel Syndrome: Towards an explanatory model. *Journal of Behavioral Medicine, 26,* 1, p. 1.

Sharma, S., Pinto, C., S Masand, P., Virk, S., Kaplan, D., Nihalani, N., & Gupta, S. (2003). Relationship of Irritable Bowel Syndrome (IBS) and major depression in Mumbai, India. *International Journal of Psychiatry in Clinical Practice, 7,* 2, p.1.

Snape, W.J., Carlson, G.M., & Cohen, S. (1976). Colonic Myloelectrical activity in the irritable bowel syndrome. *Gastroenterology, 70,* pp.326-330.

Social Model of Disability. *Wikepedia,*

http://en.wikipedia.org/wiki/Social_model_of_disability

Stress, fatigue levels determine quality of life in IBS. *Digestive Disorders,* January 2005, p. 59.

Stuttaford, Thomas (2003). Anxiety and rich food trigger IBS. *The United Kingdom Times,* 3/27/2003.

Suls, J., Wan, C., & Blanchard, E. (1994). A multilevel data-analytic approach for evaluation of relationships between daily life stressors and symptomatology: Patients with Irritable Bowel Syndrome. *Health Psychology, 13,* 2, p. 103.

Suszynski, Marie (April 2009). Getting an IBS diagnosis. *Everydayhealth.com,* p.1.

Sykes, M., Lackner, J., Keefer, L., & Krasner, S. (2003). Psychopathology in Irritable Bowel Syndrome: Support for a psychophysiological model. *Journal of Behavioral Medicine, 26,* 4, p. 361.

The UNC Center for Functional GI and Motility Disorders. http://www.med.unc.edu/medicine/fgidc/palsson.htm

Tkachuk, G., Graff, L., Martin, G., & Bernstein, C. (2003). Randomized controlled trial of cognitive-behavioral group therapy for Irritable Bowel Syndrome in medical setting.

Journal of Clinical Psychology in Medical Settings, 10, 1, pp. 57-69.

Toner, B., Segal, Z.,Emmott, S., & Myran (2000). Cognitive-Behavioral treatment of irritable bowel syndrome: The brain-Gut connection. New York: Guilford Press Book Reviews, pp.202-204.

Toner, B., Garfinkel, P., Jeejeebhoy, K., Scher, H., Shulman, D., & Di Gasbarro, I., (1991). Depression and gastrointestinal problems. *Clinician's Research Digest, 9,* 3, p. 6.

UNC Center for Functional GI & Motility Disorders. www.med.unc.edu/medicine/fgidc/research. Understanding and treating an irritable bowel. *Harvard Women's Health,11*, 8, pp.1-3.

Walters, V. & Oakley, D. (2006). Hypnotic imagery as an adjunct to therapy for Irritable Bowel Syndrome: An experimental case report. *Contemporary Hypnosis, 23,* 3, p. 141-149.

Weber, F., & McCallum, R. (1992). Clinical approaches to Irritable Bowel Syndrome. *Lancet, 340,* 8833, p.1447-1456.

www.ingramcontent.com/pod-product-compliance
Lightning Source LLC
Chambersburg PA
CBHW081236280526
45787CB00006B/2677

9781535179034